To Know Him is to Love Him

Stephanie Anderson

authorHOUSE®

AuthorHouse™
1663 Liberty Drive
Bloomington, IN 47403
www.authorhouse.com
Phone: 1-800-839-8640

First published by AuthorHouse 9/17/2009

ISBN: 978-1-4490-3012-4 (e)
ISBN: 978-1-4490-3011-7 (sc)

Printed in the United States of America
Bloomington, Indiana

This book is printed on acid-free paper.

This book is dedicated to
Joe Anderson,
the love of my life

Chapters

Acknowledgments

I have to first thank my husband for all the love and support. Joe, you have truly been a blessing to me and I hope I take the information in this book and fulfill all you wants and needs. I truly love you with all my Heart! You complete me in so many ways!

Maegan —

I continue to watch you blossom into an incredible woman and daughter. I am so proud of you and your music. Keep pushing and eventually you will break through. Your song writing and voice continues to grow with such beauty and elegance! I Love You!

Dawson —

My superman, you are such an awesome son! You are growing up so fast and you make me so proud to be your mom. I love you!

Sherrie, thank you for the incredible graphics I could not have done this book with out you! You have added so much creativity with your graphics! You always read my mind. You have made the pages come alive!

Susan, thank you for taking my crazy grammar and putting it in order. You have done such a awesome job at editing. This book would not be the same.

To Author House Publishing, thank you for believing in all the small writers and giving them a voice to touch the world.

To all the people who have thought about writing and think, not me, think again, with the love and support of family and incredibly talented people you can do it!

Graphic designer: Sherrie Evans.........
Sherrie.evans@xlcoloroftexas.com

Editor: Susan Elliot.............
The write word ske9999@swbell.net

Publisher: Authorhouse Publishing
Authorhouse.com

Introduction

This book will be one of the greatest tools you will ever possess in your relationship. It will teach you how to:

💜 Plan the perfect night
💜 Surprise your partner with Love Ideas
💜 Ignite a newfound passion you did not know existed
💜 Open up a whole new world of love and fulfillment

I wrote this book because I think it is important for couples to know and experience each other in every area of their lives.

One of the first questions people ask when I talk about the concept for *To Know Him is to Love Him* and *To Know Her is To Love Her* is, "What gave you the idea?" This inspiring idea emerged from an overwhelming desire to teach and help couples draw closer together. It comes from thinking about how wonderful it would be to have a place where all types of information about each other could be available at a moment's notice, such as:

- ♥ Likes
- ♥ Dislikes
- ♥ Favorite golf courses
- ♥ Favorite electronics
- ♥ Wish list
- ♥ ♥ ♥ and much more.

All this information could be kept in a journal of sorts, and in one place, somewhat like CliffsNotes® for couples, or cheat sheets for women.

One afternoon after my divorce, I was thinking about it and wondering, "How can I help couples stay connected? How could I help end divorces? What can I do to prevent a future divorce in my own life?"

After thinking about the last sixteen years of my marriage, I wondered what might have made a difference? What might have kept me from a divorce? I've always believed the adage, "Failure is *success* if you learn from it."

Two of the big things that I found along this journey and pathway:

1. He did not know me, and
2. Like many women, I always assumed he could read my mind, or I wanted him to.

I believe that had this book been available to me, I would not be a divorced woman right now. My marriage would have been spared.

Knowledge leads to intimacy for couples and your key to opening that lock lies within the pages of this book. Let me explain a little bit more about the creative beginnings of *To Know Him is To Love Him.*

It was approximately twelve years into my sixteen-year marriage when all hell broke loose. My husband was going out for sandwiches. He was gathering orders for the family when he came to me, I laughed and said, "You are kidding, right?"

He looked puzzled and said, "No, what kind?"

"A ham-and-cheese foot-long," I said. "We always share that."

"Okay, and what do you want on it?" he asked.

"The same as I have ordered for twelve years," I said.

"What is that?" he asked.

Here is the kicker of the story. Next he asked me if I wanted mayo or mustard. I hate mustard!

Okay, so right now you're thinking, she divorced him over mustard? No, that was the straw, or combination of things, that broke the camel's back. At this point I no longer wanted the sandwich or was even hungry — just angry.

I said, "No, what I do want is for you to know me. After twelve years, why should I have to tell you what kind of sandwich I like? I mean, if you really loved me, you would know...I hate mustard."

That is where *To Know Her is to Love Her* and *To Know Him is To Love Him* come into the picture. In these books you both will have written all your unexpressed secrets and desires to share with each other; all you have to do is read to know your partner.

Had my ex had this book, he could have ordered everything just the way I like it without asking, and let me know that he loved me at the same time. Brilliant!

Yes, of course it will take time and discipline to record your information, but oh my, what a great treasure awaits you at the end of this book.

You will learn to get up-close and personal with the man who loves you, and you will discover again the love dancing that brought you together, along with each other's likes and dislikes.

This book will be priceless to your future love life!

I don't believe anyone gets married expecting to just exist in a state of boredom. We all want to have that original loving feeling sustain us through the years. Problems develop if we allow ourselves to get into a rut of despair and are unable to function, or put any effort into our man or marriage; everything begins to disintegrate.

In this book you will find many options and opportunities to get organized and begin your new journey of communication.

Women, it is time to step up to the challenge of knowing what is on his mind and how he likes it.

Together you will learn the keys to each other's happiness. You will love the reward.

(Men, grab a copy of *To Know Her is to Love Her* to give her. I promise it will keep you out of the doghouse more than once.)

To Know Him Is To *Love* Him

Is your marriage on the road to divorce? Let me teach you how to change lanes and receive the keys to a new adventure.

Have you ever thought about why men have affairs? They lack encouragement from their partner. They need sex, sex, love, and did I say sex?

As women, we should learn to be more attractive to our guy, to encourage him, and take time to prepare ourselves for our men.

We underestimate the importance of looking sexy for our man. Trust me women, he knows your size, and any size can be sexy when you are exciting, playful, and confident. Just ask him. He needs you to be playful, sexy, and inviting.

I want to teach you how to treat your man as a king. At least once a month, give him a royal dinner in bed and a royal massage (along with control of the remote).

I want to teach you how to communicate better. (Ask questions)

I want you to learn his innermost desires. (Find out his love touches.)

 Leave him Love Notes such as: "You are my Superman."

 Learn how to have date nights that please him. (Go to the park and race remote-control cars).

 Learn to encourage him and lift him up as the king of the house.

Don't ever dishonor him at home or in public. Don't be known as the nagging wife; be known as the queen. Learn to walk like royalty. Learn to keep a smile on his face all the time.

Learn what makes him smile.

Bring back "that lovin' feeling." Trust me, he did not marry you to be bored. He married you because you made him tingle inside. Find that tingle again. As love and marriage expert Gary Chapman says, "Fill his love tank."

Women, take the challenge and serve your king. Read all about him and surprise him with love ideas like hiding tattoos all over your body and having a body hunt.

You will probably have to fill this book out for him. Ask him questions and take the time to get the answers. Your marriage will greatly benefit from it!

Thoughts for the day:

(Excerpted from *Secrets About Men Every Woman Should Know* by Barbara DeAngelis or *What Every Woman Should Know* by Bishop E. Bernard Jordan)

 Arguing without seeking solutions is a destructive game.

 Most men believe that romance and sex is the same thing.

 Romance is fun work.

 Never stop dating your husband.

 Learn to compromise rather than complain.

Every woman should know:

 A wise woman strengthens her family.

 A wife of character is her husband's crown.

 How to laugh at mistakes after the tears dry.

Sexy Says It ♥♥ ♥

Sexy says all kinds of things. And being sexy can be so simple, when you make the effort.

Women, did you know that men think about sex more than 200 times in a day! *Wow* was my thought when I read that information. I always thought and was told that men only want one thing: sex. Okay, so maybe it is true, but bottom line, men need sexual touch to feel loved. Women, on the other hand, need comfort to feel loved. We have to learn to find the right balance between each partner.

I hope that you, as women, can learn to find other things that make him happy. In this book you may be the one to ask questions and record them, but it will be worth the time and effort. Find out what makes him happy outside the bedroom and you should have a very happy man. Ask yourself if you could you buy his favorite music, his favorite golf clubs, or perhaps the latest fishing gear that would thrill him?

Would you know where to send him and the boys for a weekend away? Such a weekend could be very beneficial for you to arrange. Time alone is an amazing thing. You both should feel renewed after such a weekend.

I want you to be able to change the atmosphere in your home into a loving environment. Women say to me all the time, "But you don't know my husband!" You're right, but I have seen those same husbands who were not interested in love, find the girl who makes them smile and off they went!

If you think I'm wrong, look at why men have affairs. Or think about it, don't men get married more quickly than women after divorce? I asked myself, "Why do men jump into a relationship so quickly after being so unhappy?" That question led me to research the subject.

Men say that women tend to become their mom. (For tips on improving this problem, check out my book on *How to Transform from Mom-Mode to Wife-Mode*, coming soon.)

Men want and need to be with someone all the time, but stop and look around. How do your friends or yourself treat your partners?

Men need what I call their Man Cards back. Women take them away when we become a man's mom! Learn to find your man's strengths and encourage him. Learn to be sexy again.

I encourage you to take the challenge find out all the little things that make your man happy. Just like women, men feel loved when you do special things for them.

I think the most difficult challenge is change. How do we change the way we act? It is tough but a happy marriage is certainly worth the work. Change, change, change and you will find so much good will happen. Find the key to getting out of your rut.

Get creative and you'll be able to rock his world!

Love Ideas

Do you need some spice in your relationship, or are you bored? This section is for you. Love ideas will add spice to your life. They are different than date ideas. Most are inexpensive and only take time, thought, and love.

Take these ideas and have him pick his top 20 favorites. Ask him to update the list often so you will have new ideas from which to pick. Always have him write in pencil so you can keep new ideas coming. Tell him that if he has other ideas he would like, he can write his own or circle additional ones that he likes.

If you are short on money, you can write or print virtually anything on a love note and tell him that if you could, you would buy him the world.

This is my favorite chapter of the book because to me, these ideas spark Love Dancing 101.

I want this chapter to ignite a new passion and excitement that's probably been missing in your relationship for a long time.

The more you use this chapter, the better you will get at understanding each other. You will be a love expert in no time.

Learn to be creative and think outside the box. Personalize things as often as you can. Everybody loves seeing and hearing his own name, so when you leave him a special note be sure to include his name. For example: "_____, let's kiss and make up." It will make him laugh.

Remember to always honor each other. Never criticize each other. This is so important. Your words have the power of life and death. Unkind words can kill a marriage. You can destroy a night by one negative comment. Honor each other.

Also remember to never use sex as a bargaining tool. Women don't think of sex in the same way that men do. Women tend to think that's all men care about. I know you are probably saying that's true, but just because you do something special for her, don't expect an immediate payback.

To a woman, love and respect come from outside the bedroom. For men it comes from inside the bedroom. Remember to respect her outside the bedroom and she will learn to respect you in the bedroom. Before long, you will be doing some amazing love dancing.

Don't forget to give her a copy of *To Know Her is To Love Her*. You will find some great sexy suggestions to ignite new love passion in your life.

Love Ideas to Try

Buy a jersey of his favorite team and wear it to bed
    Or
Study a new language and use it to excite him
    Or
Use your new language to travel to a foreign city
    Or
Ask your mate to take a shower with you
    Or
Order a lingerie catalog and have him pick his favorites
    Or
Make a book about what you love about him
    Or
Make a book on what you find sexy about him
    Or
At dinner, play footsie under the table
    Or
Whisper sexy words in his ear as you serve him dinner
    Or
Whisper sexy words to him at a party as you walk by
    Or
Text him something sexy at home
    Or
Text him something sexy at a party. (Be ready to leave quickly.)
    Or
First thing in the morning, wake him up with a little
love dancing
    Or

Wake him up with breakfast in bed
Or
Have him take sexy pictures of you in lingerie and then print them yourself for his eyes only
Or
Slip him a note in his briefcase telling him how good he was last night
Or
Text him in the middle of the day and tell him you were just thinking about the amazing time you had last night
Or
Mail a sexy note to him at work
Or
Leave a trail of signs on his way to work telling him how much you love him
Or
Leave a trail of signs on Father's Day telling him what an amazing dad he is. (Have the kids get involved.)
Or
Leave a trail of signs for him just because!
Or
Decorate the garage for him. Make it a total guy space. Find out what his favorite team is!
Or
Give him a pedicure
Or
Give him a massage
Or
Get up early and get his clothes ready for work
Or
Take his car and have it cleaned
Or

Tuck love notes all over the house
    Or
Use Easter eggs to hide notes
    Or
Leave love notes in his car
    Or
Put a love note in his gas cap
    Or
Put on a sexy dress for dinner with him
    Or
Leave a note for him in the shower
    Or
Leave a note for him on the toilet paper
    Or
Leave him a lipstick kiss on the mirror
    Or
Text a love message to him
    Or
Send a love e-mail to him
    Or
Present him with a note after dinner that says, "Meet me in 5 minutes for dessert!"
    Or
Blow him a kiss from across the room
    Or
Make a love chain of compliments 30 days before his birthday telling him what a stud he is
    Or
Create a compliment jar
    Or
Create a compliment book
    Or

Create a date jar
    Or
While at dinner whisper in his ear when you go to the bathroom
how sexy he looks tonight
    Or
Build him a putting green
    Or
Create a pleasure jar with things and places you love to
be touched
    Or
Find a family saying that leaves a legacy and then frame it
    Or
Frame a favorite baseball card from his childhood
    Or
Buy him his favorite team autograph
    Or
Buy his favorite player's autograph for him
    Or
Buy him some Lego building blocks
    Or
Buy him some Lincoln Logs and build together
    Or
Dance in the rain and then undress each other in the garage
    Or
Serve him dinner in bed
    Or
Warm his towel
    Or
Buy a heart shaped cookie cutter and use it to make pancakes,
toast or cookies
    Or
Scan a favorite picture and transfer it to a pillow for him

Or

Create a love bulletin board

 Or

Mow the yard for him

 Or

Have the yard mowed for him

 Or

Give him 30 minutes to himself when he comes home from work

 Or

Give him a Saturday off to do what he wants

 Or

Give him an ear massage

 Or

Make love magnets complimenting him in all kinds of ways

 Or

Write a thank you note to him for all he does

 Or

Iron his clothes

 Or

Stick extra money in his briefcase and tell him to go buy something he wants

 Or

Buy him a gift card and hide it somewhere. (How about hiding a Home Depot card in the garage?) It's the little things in life that make ya smile!

 Or

If he's a neat freak, clean the bathroom counter off occasionally

 Or

Have a baby wipes warmer next to the bed so after love dancing you can clean him up

Or

Keep a heated lotion dispenser next to the bed so you can give a great massage

Or

Carve a love note into the butter

Or

Carve a love note into the ice cream

Or

Wrap a note around the hot sauce telling him he is way hotter than this

Or

Be creative with notes on food in the fridge or pantry

Or

Write your love initials on the soap: "S loves J"

Or

Write on the soap: "You can suds me up anytime"

Or

Send index cards to his friends and family asking for compliments about him; compile them in a book

Or

Give him a sports basket for TV watching with a cool new remote, some peanuts, and even some beer if he drinks

Or

Leave him a note in lipstick that says, "I'm sorry. Let's kiss and make up."

Or

Leave him chocolate kisses with notes attached

Or

Give him a subscription to his favorite magazine and tell him he can have 30 minutes once a month on a morning to read it uninterrupted

Or

Find interesting facts about the year he was born. Men love history.

Or

Leave him a jar of nuts with a note that says, "I'm nuts about you!"

Or

Start a love journal: pass it back and forth; tell him things you love about him

Or

Make a CD for him and leave it in the car (with songs like "Wild thing, I think I love you").

Or

Create a special way or code to say "I love you" (maybe three winks, a word, or three hand squeezes)

Or

Join him in the shower for a quickie in the morning or ask him to shower before bed

Or

Buy him a guitar and a DVD that teaches how to play it

Or

Make a time capsule of your dating and bring it out on your 10-year anniversary

Or

Tuck some panties in his lunch and tell him you'll be waiting for him tonight

Or

Load a tool belt with lotions and tell him you will be his tool girl tonight

Or

Give him a gift card for car washes. (Tell him he drives you crazy and you want him to know how much.)

Or

Leave him a box of red hot candies and tell him you still think
he is red hot
    Or
Put a lipstick kiss on the newspaper for him to find
    Or
Always, always flirt with your partner
    Or
Say or do something sexy so that he will think of you often
    Or
Guys like a challenge. Keep him guessing what will you
do next.
    Or
Make one day every month when he is king for the day (for
example, the first of every month)
    Or
Buy him that new golf club he has been wanting
    Or
Make him a casserole and write, "I love you" or "stud"
with cheese
    Or
Wear a skirt to dinner with nothing on under it and whisper in
his ear at dinner to let him know. (Just don't pull a Britney!!)
    Or
Take a cold shower when you're tired and it will rejuvenate you
so you can give him some amazing love dancing!
    Or
Install a colored light bulb in the room and switch it on
frequently. They say blue makes women look softer and sexier

Words Can Last A Lifetime!

Write Your Top Love Ideas For Her

Use pencil to make your list and update it often

1. _____

2. _____

3. _____

4. _____

5. _____

6. _____

7. _____

8. _____

9. _____

10. _____

11. _____

12. _____

13. _____

14. _____

15. _____

16. _____

17. _____

18. _____

19. _____

20. _____

Great Date Ideas

Okay, women. Here is your chance to show them boys how it's done!

Sometimes we think dating is just for women but in reality, men need attention and lots of it. Become creative. Most of the time you could plan a great night at home and he would be happy with a good meal and some love dancing.

Try to think of guy things to do. For example, take him out for crab legs and learn how to be sexy when you eat them.

Buy remote-control boats, take them to the park and race them. Finish with some quiet time together.

Try to plan at least one date a month that he will like. Be spontaneous. Surprise him often with love ideas, love notes, or a date night.

Read him the list of date ideas and ask him to say yes or no for those he likes. Write the info down on his top dates and there you have it. Simple, user friendly, and he really didn't have to do much. He will reap the fringe benefits of this project.

How much easier can it get? Before you know it, he will be smiling all the time.

People will wonder what happened to him. (I know, his Love tank is finally full!)

Just like women, men need encouraging words. They need to feel loved, needed, and wanted! That is truly the key to an affair-proof marriage. Men will go where they feel needed, wanted, or loved.

Rock his world. Don't let the girl at the office have a chance!

Men need sexy. Sexiness sells everything around us! Remember, it's not the size, it's how you carry yourself.

We all have a good quality about us and we can all learn how to be sexy for our man.

You can learn to talk sexy in the bedroom and blow his mind! Don't get me wrong; I don't mean trashy but sexy. Use soothing words, encouraging words. Tell him how you feel. This can be very difficult at first, but take baby steps. Use simple words. Tell him what you're doing so he will be encouraging.

I've said it before: don't ever expect him to read your mind.

Date Ideas to Try

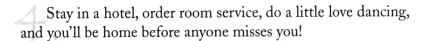

1. Find a park and race remote-control cars

2. Race remote-controlled airplanes

3. Fly kites

4. Stay in a hotel, order room service, do a little love dancing, and you'll be home before anyone misses you!

5. Stay in a hotel for the weekend

6. Set your room up for a night of massages: use a tool belt to hold different lotions; bring a basket of luscious fruits; blindfold him and let him guess what you have in mind. Be creative. Feed him.

7. Go to the movies and smooch in the back like you did when you were teenagers

8. Go night fishing. Don't forget the flashlights. Bring candles and dessert

9. Have a home improvement date. Do that remodeling project together.

10. Take him to a sporting event and rent the sign to tell him you love him more today than ever

11. Have a sundae party. Become playful with the whipped cream.

Carry it into the bedroom along with the sundae. Feed each other slowly and sensually.

12. Find a local park with a pond and bring remote-control boats. Bring a book and sit and enjoy each other's company.

13. Plan a festive theme night such as Mexican or Japanese, and dress the part. Make sure you dress sexy. He will think he is with a different exotic girl.

14. Plan a beach night and wear that itsy bitsy bikini you wouldn't dare wear out of the house. Trust me, he will love it. It's not the size, it's the sexiness that turns them on!

15. Take him to get a new suit for a nice dinner and tell him how sexy he looks

16. Buy a metal detector and have a treasure hunt

17. Play a game of miniature golf

18. Ride go-carts together

19. Go to the batting cages

20. Have a pizza night and make your own gourmet version. Be playful, flirt a little.

21. Go on a helicopter ride

22. Take a train ride together

23. Go to the horse races

Go to the car races

Find a local campsite and spend the night

Go to the aquarium

Try sushi

Go to a junk yard

Learn to scuba dive

Learn to ski

Take a dinner cruise

Be spontaneous. Go to a casino even if it takes a drive

Play Bingo

Play paint ball

Take a golf lesson

Go to a shooting range

Take a hot air balloon ride

Go skydiving

Go bungie jumping

Rent an RV

41. Rent a sports car

42. Rent a convertible

43. Have a costume party in the summer

44. Have a fondue night and feed each other

45. Rent a houseboat

46. Rent watercrafts for the day

47. Put butcher paper or a shower curtain on the kitchen floor and body paint

48. Have a game night. For example, try sexy Scrabble (try to find sexy words or things to spell)

49. Go hiking

50. Plan a bike ride

51. Play charades

52. Serve him dinner in bed. Rock his world.

53. Plan a night in wearing only his white button-down shirt to dinner

54. Meet for coffee before work

55. Meet for breakfast before work

Go to a foreign film

Surprise him with tickets to his favorite sporting event

Take him out for crab legs and learn to eat them sexy. He will love you for it

Write Your Top Date Ideas For Her

Write in pencil and make changes often

1. _____

2. _____

3. _____

4. _____

5. _____

6. _____

7. _____

8. _____

9. _____

10. _____

11. _____

12. _____

13. _____

14. _____

15. _____

16. _____

17. _____

18. _____

19. _____

20. _____

Write Your Own Love Notes

This chapter is designed to help you write your own love notes.

Go to a local office supply store and buy all shapes and sizes of Post-it® Notes. If you haven't seen self-stick notes in a while, you will be surprised at all the variety available. They come in all shapes and sizes, and in any color you could want.

Leave him love notes at least three times a week. Be creative. Take my ideas and expand on them. Add your own flair.

You may think once a week is enough for a love note but it's not.

Let me explain. You could leave him a love note, call him a couple of times during the day, but just before you leave the office a problem arises. You come home and don't talk because you need some time to unwind.

Sensing your mood, he might react by thinking you are mad at him, or that you only called him and left him a note because you felt guilty. You may be saying, "That's crazy." This is where women don't understand men.

Like you, men need encouragement. When you need time to yourself, kiss him and tell him how much you love him Ask for some time to unwind, take your time, and then thank him for being understanding. This will work much better than retreating into silence with no explanation. This is true for men and women.

Love Note Ideas

1. Why don't you try and score a touchdown tonight?

2. Got some? Want some?

3. Have you scored a goal lately? How about scoring one on me!

4. I want you.

5. I'm sorry. Can we kiss and make up?

6. Just because I love you!

7. Love you a latte!

8. Just because you are special!

9. Take me. I'm yours!

10. I love you. I love your smile. I love the way you tease me. I love it when you whisper in my ear. I love the way you love me.

11. When I think about you, stuff tingles.

12. When I think about you, my heart beats like a thousand drums.

13. would do anything for you.

14. You are my everything.

15. Want to make out?

16. For going above and beyond, thank you.

17. I love everything about you.

18. You are my favorite pillow.

19. You are my favorite hot spot.

20. Your love adds spice to my life.

21. I have written your name on my book of love in permanent marker.

22. You're one in a million for a million and one reasons.

23. You are hotter than a HEMI® engine.

You are my favorite flavor.

You are the brightest star. I could spot you anywhere.

You melt better than chocolate.

You are my chocolate chip.

Oh, the things you do to me! When can you do them again?

I want you and I enjoy needing you.

Bring the "Do not disturb" sign.

Want to get frisky?

Love muffin, honey bun, cupcake, sweetie pie. You are my favorite treat.

You don't have a clue how SEXY you really are.

You are my Stud.

I will always love you, honor you, and adore you.

I love loving you.

You are my sunshine.

Everyday I fall in love with you again

Grrrrrrr. Mmm mmm good

You are my love.

I just thought I couldn't love you more and then a new day comes and I Love You more.

I am yours, all yours. Can you handle that?

I'm so blessed to have you to snuggle, cuddle, kiss, and hug with.

I'd brake for you.

You are the only scent I crave.

Let's take a ride on the wild side.

You mean more to me than you will ever know.

I wished upon a star and there you were.

Got love? Need some, want some?

Do you want to date me?

I'd love to kiss you all over.

You are the wings that make me soar.

You're looking so good today.

You still have it and I still want it.

You complete me.

Just when life started to get dull, you added a rainbow of color to my life.

Do you like baseball? I'll let you run my bases.

Do you want to play doctor?

Let's double dip tonight.

I would follow you down any road.

Remember always, you are loved.

You are the song my heart sings all day.

You can float your marshmallows in my hot chocolate anytime.

You are my Love Boat.

You are my super star.

You can top my sundae anytime.

You are the love of my life.

You complete me.

My world got brighter the day you stepped into it.

I am glad you were my last first kiss.

Have I told you lately that you still take my breath away?

72. I love you more than the day we met.

73. You sho' nuff make me happy!

74. Everyday that I wake up with you recharges my battery.

Write Your Top Love Note Suggestions

1. _____

2. _____

3. _____

4. _____

5. _____

6. _____

7. _____

8. _____

9. _____

10. _____

11. _____

12. _____

13. _____

14. _____

15. _____

16. _____

17. _____

18. _____

19. _____

20. _____

Write Your Own
Love Coupons

Just like writing your own love notes, you can write your own love coupons.

Try to print some of these on your computer. Personalize them whenever you can for something that you know he will like.

Write his name on them. He will know that you really care when it is written just for him.

Be respectful. Don't ever disrespect each other. Never give expecting something in return.

When you learn to give from your heart, you will receive the greatest reward. (How about some of the best love dancing that you have ever had?)

Love Coupon Ideas

This coupon is good for:

1. A royal night out.

2. A royal night in.

3. A day of golf

4. A day of whatever you want.

5. A weekend of hunting.

6. A free dishwashing.

7. TV all to yourself.

8. Your turn to pick the movie.

9. A day to yourself.

10. A massage for ___ minutes.

11. A love touch anywhere you would like.

12. A morning to sleep in.

13. A nap anytime you need it.

14. Dinner in bed.

15. Breakfast in bed.

16. A day of shopping.

17. "King for the day."

18. A trip to Home Depot

19. Your choice of date idea or love idea.

20. A three-wish day.

21. A weekend away of your choice.

22. A trip to Bass Pro Shop.

This coupon is good for

A Royal Night Out

Redeemable: TONIGHT

Love,
ME

Sports &
Outdoors

Ok guys, this is for all the different boys out there. Some like outdoors and some like sports, some like computers and some like horses. So, I have designed this chapter to accommodate all your likes and dislikes.

If it doesn't apply to you leave it blank but think about it, all of these are manly things, you just might like something new and adventurous. That is the purpose of this book to excite a newness in your life, to give you that spring in your step, to let her Rock Your World.:)

If you have a different passion, scratch out anyone of my ideas and

46

add your own, Remember this book is all about you and the more information you give her the better it will be.

This book is not designed to be neat and perfect im talking mark all through it, change it make it all about you.

ENJOY!!!!!

Teach her, talk to her, and let her Rock Your World!!!

Women;
When your partner is out doing his favorite hobbies, sport or outdoor event, take the time to have a beauty night or day! This is a perfect opportunity to do a facial, a home pedicure, a home spa treatment or that crazy beauty mask that looks really scarey. Kinda like the saying never let them see you sweat, never let them see you at your scariest. Make him think your just naturally beautiful. There are all kinds of information online for home spa treatments. Or have you ever looked at the models in the magazine and loved their make up, Try it! When know ones home this is the perfect opportunity to try all kinds of fun things. Take a bath set the mood of relaxation and tranquility. Have a glass of wine, if you don't drink use the wine glass anyways, there is just something fun about drinking in a great glass. Get a great book and if the kids are home tell them you need 1 hour to refresh. It will make you feel renewed and refreshed!

Fishing

- ❤ Rods_____
- ❤ Reels _____
- ❤ Lures _____
- ❤ _____
- ❤ _____

Hunting

- ❤ Deer_____
- ❤ Birds _____
- ❤ Ammunition _____
- ❤ Guns_____
- ❤ Collectors items _____
- ❤ _____
- ❤ _____

Golf

- ❤ Clubs _____
- ❤ Balls_____
- ❤ Tee Size_____
- ❤ _____
- ❤ _____

Don't question him to much,
be his wife, not his mother!

Skiing

1._____
2._____
3._____
4._____
5._____

Football

1._____
2._____
3._____
4._____
5._____

Baseball

♥ Balls_____
♥ Bat_____
♥ Shoes_____
♥ Size_____
♥ _____
♥ _____

Basketball

♥ Ball_____
♥ Shorts_____
♥ Size_____

♥ Shoes_____
♥ Size_____
♥ _____
♥ _____

Computers

♥ Brand_____
♥ Software _____
♥ Disc _____
♥ _____
♥ _____

Music

♥ Stores _____
♥ Equipment _____
♥ _____
♥ _____

Racing

♥ Gear _____
♥ Equipment _____
♥ _____
♥ _____

Horses

♥ Gear_____
♥ Saddle _____

❤ Clothes _____
❤ Sizes _____
❤ Boots _____
❤ Sizes _____
❤ _____
❤ _____

Hobbies

1. _____
2. _____
3. _____
4. _____
5. _____

Camping

❤ Gear _____
❤ _____
❤ _____

Outdoor

1. _____
2. _____
3. _____
4. _____
5. _____

Surprise him often!

Biking

1._____
2._____
3._____
4._____
5._____

Misc

1._____
2._____
3._____
4._____
5._____

Remember ♥ ♥ ♥

Men need to fill like men
Men need hobbies
Men need friends
Men need time alone

How to
Know Me . . .

This chapter will provide important information about his sizes — jeans as well as dres pants — so that when you want to plan an amazing night out you can buy him a new outfit.

You may think that most guys wouldn't want or care about new clothes, but you just might be surprised. How good do you feel in a new outfit? Everyone likes the way they look in new clothes. And in today's society, men love new clothes as much, if not more, than women.

Find out whether he likes gold or silver jewelry, or whether he would even wear a bracelet. Think about getting new cuff links for him. Neck sizes are important for guys' clothing. Do you know his size?

How about a selecting a new necktie for him? Does he prefer bold, classic, or simple styling?

Learn what kind of fishing he likes: bass or trout?

Learn his favorite golf courses — the ones he would love to play if they weren't so expensive. Call and see if they offer special rates or certain discount days. Or, if you have extra money, call his buddy and pay the greens fees for both of them.

How much more special would he feel if you said. "Hey honey, I love you so much that I called Jeff and paid for you to have a great day of golf together." Or maybe you should go play golf with him. Which choice do you think would make him smile?

Personalizing your gifts makes him feel like you cared enough to go through the trouble of booking him a great day.

And while he's out, find a babysitter for the night and prepare the house for a great romantic meal and some love dancing (if you know what I mean). He will think about you all week long.

That is the goal of this book: to be on his mind all the time so that when someone asks him about his wife, all he can do is smile because his love tank is overflowing!

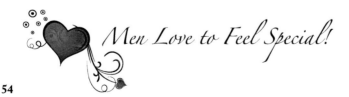 *Men Love to Feel Special!*

 The Basics

My birthday/ birthstone _____

Anniversary_____

Special day_____

Important Names and Numbers
- Florist _____
- Ticketmaster _____
- Hair Salon _____
- Nail Salon _____
- Massage _____
- Tanning Salon _____

Favorite Stores/Destinations
- Clothes _____
- Shoes _____
- Jewelry (gold or silver?)_____
- Home improvement _____
- Favorite computer store _____
- Favorite golf courses _____

Treats
- Magazine _____
- Candy _____
- Soda _____
- Coffee _____
- Pizza _____
- Take-out _____

- 💜 Dinner _____
- 💜 Pie _____
- 💜 Cake _____

My Sizes

Ask him to go to a jeweler to determine his ring size. Tell him to be specific. Have him get measurements for both his right and left hand. Ask for wrist measurements also, so that you can have a watch or bracelet sized before you give it to him. (You might need to go with him so he doesn't feel silly. Do it together.)

Have him go to a suit store for his exact clothing measurements. You will need this information someday.

Remember, after you have this information, use it. Make sure your gifts are the right size before you give him something and if it's not right, make it right.

My ex once bought me a bracelet in the airport. The store only had a large size bracelet so he bought it anyway, even though he knew it wouldn't fit. He gave the bracelet to me and said, "You will have to send it off and have it re-sized." I remember thinking, "How thoughtless of him, buying me a gift just to say he did, and then telling me to send it off."

I left the bracelet on the counter with the jeweler's address, determined not to have it sized or sent off. I thought, "Why should I have to send it off? He should do it."

Needless to say, I never sent it off and it never got done. The more I looked at that bracelet the more I hated it. It reminded me of how much he cared, or didn't. So remember, you hold the key to his happiness with the actions you take.

My Sizes

💜 Ring
💜 Wrist measurement
💜 Necklace length
💜 Watch

Shirt sizes

💜 Short sleeve
💜 Button-up
💜 Neck size
💜 T-shirt
💜 Pants
💜 Shorts
💜 Jacket
💜 Sweats

Shoe Size

💜 Golf shoe
💜 Tennis shoes
💜 Boots
💜 Sock size
💜 Underwear size
💜 Boxers

I prefer:

Circle the ones you love

I Like

Roses, daisies, orchids

Sweats or Shorts

Boxers or Briefs

T-shirt or Polo

Massage or Playful

Shoes or Purses

Belts or Socks

SUV or Sedan

Sports Car or Mini-Van

Outlet Mall or Antiques Shop

Concert or Jazz Bar

Opera or Play

Home Depot or Lowe's

Pool or Darts

Inside or Outside

Grill out or Take-out

Dark Chocolate or Milk Chocolate

Pizza or Chinese

American Cheese or Swiss Cheese

White or Wheat Bread

Mayonnaise or Mustard

Cake or Pie

Brownies or Cupcakes

Game Boards or Electronics

Cards or Dominoes

Golf or Basketball

Fishing or Hunting

Baseball or Football

Snow or Beach

Book or Magazine

Christian Music or Rock

Country Music or Soul

Wheels: Chrome or Alloy

Cologne or Spray

Family Photograph or Painting

TV or Movie

Lotion or Body Gel

Favorite Foods and Restaurants
Favorite restaurants, directions and phone numbers

Fancy
1._____
2._____
3._____
4._____
5._____

Casual
1. _____

2._____
3._____
4._____
5._____

Take-out favorites

Pizza _____

Chinese _____

Italian _____

BBQ _____

Mexican _____

Top 5 take-out restaurants

1._____
2._____
3._____
4._____
5._____

Favorite fast food   ♥

Taco Bell_____

Wendy's _____

McDonalds_____

1._____
2._____
3._____
4._____
5._____

Favorite Candy

1._____
2._____
3._____
4._____
5._____

❤❤❤ Time to Myself ❤❤❤
If I had a day in, I would like:

To be by myself _____
Lie around and do nothing _____
A home project _____
1._____
2._____
3._____
4._____

If I had time to myself I would like to:
Watch a Movie _____
Read a book _____
Sleep in _____

I would love to get breakfast in bed or to have breakfast prepared for me.
My favorite breakfast is:
1._____
2._____
3._____
4._____

If I had a Day Out, I would like to Shop for:

Antiques _____

Houses _____

Cars _____

Camping Gear _____

1. _____
2. _____
3. _____
4. _____
5. _____

Special Things I Love:

1. _____
2. _____
3. _____
4. _____
5. _____
6. _____
7. _____
8. _____
9. _____
10. _____

Favorite Electronic Stuff

Computer _____

Camera _____

Phone _____

Sound/music equipment _____

Jewelry choices

Bracelet

1._____

2._____

Necklace

1._____

2._____

Ring

1._____

2._____

I like
Gold or Silver

1._____

2._____

3._____

Favorite jewelry stores

1._____
2._____
3._____
4._____
5._____

Favorite Vacations

If I could go on vacations I would like:

Snow   Beach   Mountains   Wine country

1._____

2._____

3._____

If I could go on a weekend getaway

In town (see local hotels) _____

Within 100 miles _____

Within 200 miles _____

Things to pack for me:

Clothes _____

Cleansers_____

Hair Products _____

Miscellaneous must-haves

1._____

2._____

3._____

Destination Ideas

Hawaii   France   Italy

Las Vegas   The Bahamas   Quebec

Mexico   Banff   Oregon

Florida   Colorado   Greece

My Favorite Destinations

1._____

2._____

3._____

4._____

5._____

Favorite Local Hotels
Has a Spa, heated pool, restaurant, or bar.
Directions and phone numbers.

1._____

2._____

3._____

4._____

5._____

It's not the thought that counts,
it's knowing his thoughts that count!

My Wish List
(Write in pencil & update frequently)

1. _____

2. _____

3. _____

4. _____

5. _____

6. _____

7. _____

8. _____

9. _____

10. _____

11. _____

12. _____

13. _____

14. _____

15. _____

16. _____

17. _____

18. _____

19. _____

20. _____

*"Love is Learning to Give
even when You Want to Receive!"*

"Love is Complimenting, Not Criticizing."

*"Breath often,
Love will take Your Breathe Away!"*

Question & Answers

This chapter is for fun. Just some crazy questions to help you know him a little better. Take the information, have fun, and add some of your own questions. Remember, this chapter is designed to know him and to know him is to love him.

What was the happiest day of your life?

_____

Have you ever met a celebrity? Who?

_____

If you could do any job in the world, what would you do?

_____

If you could change anything about yourself, what would it be?

_____

What's your favorite memory?

_____

What's your favorite type of music?

_____

Do you have a favorite band?

_____

What's your most beloved possession?

_____

What's your favorite movie?

_____

If you had a million dollars, what would you do with it?

_____

Who do you think is the sexiest actress?

_____

What's your favorite love song?

_____

If you could change places with anyone, who would it be and why?

_____

If you could eat only one food for the rest of your life, what would
it be?

_____

What is your favorite animal?

_____

If you could have any animal for a pet, what would it be?

_____

What person do you admire the most?

_____

Who was your favorite school teacher?

_____

What's the most romantic date you have ever had?

_____

What is the funniest memory you have?

_____

Where was your fist kiss, and with who?

_____

What was the most embarrassing moment of your life?

_____

What is your favorite sports team?

_____

Did you play sports as a kid? If yes, what kind?

_____

Did you ever want to be a superstar? When and why?

_____

As a kid, who did you want to marry ?

_____

Do you believe in God?

_____

Do you believe in angels?

_____

Would you like to travel into outer space?

_____

If you could have any car you wanted, what would it be?

_____

Who is your favorite family member, and why?

_____

Who do you think taught you the most?

_____

What would you change if you were president?

_____

I really like when she wears her hair:
        ♥ Curly   ♥ Straight   ♥ Permed
        ♥ Short   ♥ Long

I like when she wears:
        ♥ A Dress ♥ Shorts   ♥ Jeans   ♥ _____

I think you're sexy when you _____

I like when you _____

Your greatest strength to me is_____

When I look at you, I remember what made me fall in love

with you: _____

5 things I love about my girl:

1._____

2._____

3._____

4._____

5._____

You make me smile when you: _____

The best kiss you ever gave me was: _____

I wish you said _____more.

My favorite gift you gave me was: _____

I love the little things you do for me, such as: _____

I would love to travel to _____

Id like to retire in or on_____

I am (circle the ones that apply)
- 💜 messy
- 💜 clean
- 💜 loud
- 💜 quiet
- 💜 silly
- 💜 serious
- 💜 competitive
- 💜 free-spirited

Favorite movie quote: _____

Favorite movies: _____

What I love about the movies: _____

When I watch them I feel: _____

I always cry when I watch: _____

I always laugh when I watch: _____

Favorite TV shows: _____

What I love about them: _____

Favorite books: _____

Favorite snack food: _____

- 💜 Morning _____

💜 Night_____

💜 Bedtime snack_____

Favorite games _____

Favorite holiday_____

I love the smell of
   💜 in my home _____
   💜 cologne _____
   💜 perfume _____
   💜 lotion _____
   💜 bath scent _____

I love weather when it is
   💜 cold
   💜 hot
   💜 rainy
   💜 snow

Favorite cartoon as a kid_____

Favorite commercial: _____

My hidden talent: _____

One of my favorite dates with you was: _____

Our most romantic date: _____

Our most unusual date: _____

Our worst date: _____

Every time I hear this song _____ I think of you

Places I love to shop: _____

My favorite color: _____

Favorite/lucky Number: _____

Hobbies: _____

Favorite animal: _____

Names, addresses, and e-mails
Directions and phone numbers:

Babysitters

1._____

2._____

3._____

Memories are priceless,
make lots of them!

Family

Mom _____

Dad _____

Sister(s) _____

Brother(s) _____

Grandpa _____

Grandma _____

In-laws

Mom _____

Dad _____

Sister(s) _____

Brother (s) _____

Grandpa _____

Grandma _____

My Top Buddies

1. _____
2. _____
3. _____
4. _____
5. _____
6. _____
7. _____
8. _____
9. _____
10. _____

"I believe the key to a happy marriage is to have fun!"

Important Numbers
To Know

What other contacts are important for her to have?
Add them below:

1._____

2._____

3._____

4._____

5._____

6._____

7._____

8._____

9._____

10. _____

His Journal

83

Her Journal

Notes

Use these pages for capturing important facts about your guy. When you hear him say he would like to have or do something, this is where you write it down. Record those wishes and make them come true.

When you go shopping, take this book with you. It now holds all the important information you need to know. No more puzzling over what he might like or what will fit. You should be able to find the answers in these pages.

Notes

 Notes

Notes

Notes

Notes

Notes